Born in 1937

by

Kerry Butters.

Born in 1937

Millennium:	**2nd millennium**
Centuries:	19th century – **20th century** – 21st century
Decades:	1900s 1910s 1920s – **1930s** – 1940s 1950s 1960s
Years:	1934 1935 1936 – **1937** – 1938 1939 1940

1937 (MCMXXXVII) was a common year starting on Friday (dominical letter C) of the Gregorian calendar, the 1937th year of the Common Era (CE) and *Anno Domini* (AD) designations, the 937th year of the 2nd millennium, the 37th year of the 20th century, and the 8th year of the 1930s decade.

Contents

Events

January

- January 1 – Anastasio Somoza García becomes President of Nicaragua.
- January 11 – The first issue of *Look* magazine goes on sale in the United States.
- January 19 – Spanish Civil War: Second Battle of the Corunna Road (begun 13 December 1936) concludes with both sides withdrawing.
- January 19 – Howard Hughes establishes a record by flying from Los Angeles to New York City in 7 hours, 28 minutes and 25 seconds.
- January 20 – Franklin D. Roosevelt is sworn in as President of the United States for a second term by Chief Justice Charles Evans Hughes. This is the first time Inauguration Day in the United States is on this date, on which continues to occur; the change is due to the ratification in 1933 of the Twentieth Amendment to the United States Constitution.
- January 23 – Moscow Trials: Trial of the Anti-Soviet Trotskyist Center – In the Soviet Union seventeen leading Communists go on trial, accused of participating in a plot led by Leon Trotsky to overthrow Joseph Stalin's regime and assassinate its leaders.

- January 26 – Michigan celebrates its centennial anniversary as a U.S. state.
- January 31 – The Soviet Union executes 31 people for alleged Trotskyism.

January 19: Howard Hughes sets record.

February

- February 5 – U.S President Franklin D. Roosevelt proposes a plan to enlarge the Supreme Court of the United States.
- February 8 – Spanish Civil War: Falangist troops take Málaga.
- February 8 – February 27 – Spanish Civil War – Battle of Jarama: Nationalist and government troops fight to a stalemate.
- February 11 – A sit-down strike ends when General Motors recognizes the United Automobile Workers union.
- February 16 – Wallace H. Carothers receives a patent for nylon.
- February 19
  - Airliner VH-UHH (*Stinson*) goes down over Lamington National Park, bound for Sydney, killing five people.
  - Yekatit 12: During a public ceremony at the Viceregal Palace (the former Imperial residence) in Addis Ababa, Ethiopia, two Eritrean nationalists attempt to kill viceroy Rodolfo Graziani with a number of grenades. The Italian security guard fire into the crowd of Ethiopian onlookers. Authorities exact further reprisals, which include indiscriminately slaughtering native Ethiopians over the next three days, detaining thousands of Ethiopians at Danan and slaughtering almost 300 monks at Debre Libanos monastery.
- The flag of the Netherlands is officially adopted.

- February 20 – Roberto Ortiz is elected president of Argentina.
- February 21 – The League of Nations Non-Intervention Committee prohibits foreign nationals from fighting in the Spanish Civil War.

March

- March – The first issue of *Detective Comics* is published in the United States. It goes on to become the longest continually published comic book in American history; it is still published as of 2015.
- March 10 (dated March 14 (Passion Sunday)) – The encyclical *Mit brennender Sorge* ("With burning concern") of Pope Pius XI is published in Germany in the German language. Largely the work of Cardinals von Faulhaber and Pacelli, it condemns breaches of the 1933 Reichskonkordat agreement signed between the Nazi government and the Catholic Church, and criticises Nazism's views on race and other matters incompatible with Catholicism.
- March 17 – The Atherton Report (private investigator Edwin Atherton's report detailing vice and police corruption in San Francisco) is released.
- March 18 – New London School explosion: In the worst school disaster in American history in terms of lives lost, the New London School in New London, Texas, suffers a catastrophic natural gas explosion, killing in excess of 295 students and teachers. Mother Frances Hospital opens in Tyler, Texas, a day ahead of schedule in response to the explosion.
- March 19 – The encyclical *Divini Redemptoris* of Pope Pius XI, critical of communism, is published.
- March 21
  - Ponce massacre: A police squad, acting under orders from Governor of Puerto Rico Blanton Winship, opens fire on demonstrators protesting at the arrest of Puerto Rican Nationalist Party leader Pedro Albizu Campos, killing 17 people and injuring over 200.
  - The first successful flying car, Waldo Waterman's *Aerobile*, makes its initial flight.
  -

- March 26
  - In Crystal City, Texas, spinach growers erect a statue of the cartoon character Popeye.
  - William H. Hastie becomes the first African American appointed to a federal judgeship in the United States.

April

- April 1
  - Aden becomes a British crown colony.
  - Bombing of Jaén in Spain by the Condor Legion of the Nazi German Luftwaffe.
- April 9 – The *Kamikaze* arrives at Croydon Airport in London; it is the first Japanese-built aircraft to fly to Europe.
- April 12
  - Frank Whittle ground-tests the world's first jet engine designed to power an aircraft, at Rugby, England.
  - *NLRB v. Jones & Laughlin Steel Corp.*: The Supreme Court of the United States rules that the National Labor Relations Act is constitutional.
- April 17 – The animated short *Porky's Duck Hunt*, directed by Tex Avery for the Looney Tunes series, featuring the debut of Daffy Duck, is released in the United States.
- April 20 – A fire in an elementary school in Kilingi-Nõmme, Estonia, kills seventeen students and injures fifty.
- April 26 – Spanish Civil War: Bombing of Guernica in Spain by the Condor Legion of the Nazi German Luftwaffe in support of the Francoists. Three-quarters of the town is destroyed and hundreds killed.

May

May 6: The *Hindenburg* disaster occurs.

- May
  - The Dáil Éireann passes the Executive Authority (Consequential Provisions) Act, 1937, which abolishes the office of Governor-General of the Irish Free State, retrospectively dated to December 1936.
  - 17 million unemployed in the USA.
- May 1 – A general strike occurs in Paris, France.
- May 6 – *Hindenburg* disaster: In the United States, the German airship *Hindenburg* bursts into flame when mooring to a mast in Lakehurst, New Jersey. Of the 36 passengers and 61 crew on board, 13 passengers and 22 crew die, as well as one member of the ground crew.
- May 7 – Spanish Civil War: The German Condor Legion Fighter Group, equipped with Heinkel He 51 biplanes, arrives in Spain to assist Francisco Franco's forces.
- May 12 – The coronation of King George VI and Queen Elizabeth takes place at Westminster Abbey, London.
- May 21
  - A Soviet station becomes the first scientific research settlement to operate on the drift ice of the Arctic Ocean.
  - As one of the reprisals for the attempted assassination of Italian viceroy Rodolfo Graziani, a detachment of Italian troops massacres the entire community of Debre Libanos, killing 297 monks and 23 laymen.
- May 27 – In California, the Golden Gate Bridge opens to pedestrian traffic, creating a vital link between San Francisco and

Marin County. The next day, President Franklin D. Roosevelt pushes a button in Washington, D.C., signaling the start of vehicle traffic over the bridge.
- May 28 – Neville Chamberlain becomes Prime Minister of the United Kingdom.
- May 28 – In Germany Volkswagen Group is founded, to build a "people's car". A new town is set to be created to house the thousands of workers who will be involved in the production of the car.
- May 30
  - Spanish Civil War: Spanish ship *Ciudad de Barcelona* is torpedoed.
  - The Chicago Police Department shoot and kill ten unarmed demonstrators in Chicago in what is known as the Memorial Day massacre.

June

- June 3 – Wallis Simpson marries The Duke of Windsor (the former Edward VIII), in France.
- June 8
  - The first total solar eclipse to exceed seven minutes of totality in over 800 years, is visible in the Pacific and Peru.
  - Carl Orff's *Carmina Burana* premieres in Frankfurt, Germany.
- June 14 – Pennsylvania becomes the first (and only) of the United States to celebrate Flag Day officially as a state holiday.
- June 21 – The coalition government of Léon Blum resigns in France.
- June – Picasso completes his painting *Guernica*.
- June/July – The Dáil Éireann debates and passes the draft new Constitution of Ireland, which is then submitted for public approval by plebiscite.

July

- July 1
  - The Gestapo arrests pastor Martin Niemöller in Germany.
  - In a referendum the people of the Irish Free State accept the new Constitution by 685,105 votes to 527,945.
  - First alleged sighting of the White River Monster.
- July 2
  - Amelia Earhart and navigator Fred Noonan disappear after taking off from New Guinea during Earhart's attempt to become the first woman to fly around the world.
  - A guard takes his place at the Tomb of the Unknowns in Washington, D.C.; continuous guard has been maintained there ever since.
- July 4 – *The Lost Colony* historical drama is first performed at an outdoor theater in the location where it is set, Roanoke Island, North Carolina.
- July 5
  - The canned precooked meat product Spam is introduced by the Hormel company in the United States
  - The highest recorded temperature in Canada, at Yellow Grass, Saskatchewan, is 45 °C (113 °F).
- July 7
  - Sino-Japanese War: Battle of Lugou Bridge (aka Marco Polo Bridge Incident): Japanese forces invade China (often seen as the beginning of World War II in Asia).
  - Peel Commission proposes partition of the British Mandate of Palestine into separate Arab and Jewish states.
- July 9 – The silent film archives of Fox Film Corporation are destroyed by the 1937 Fox vault fire.
- July 11 – American popular composer George Gershwin dies in Los Angeles of a brain tumor, age 38.
- July 20 – The Geibeltbad Pirna is opened in Dresden, Germany.

- July 21 – Éamon de Valera is elected President of the Executive Council (prime minister) of the Irish Free State by the Dáil (parliament).
- July 22 – New Deal: The United States Senate votes down President Franklin D. Roosevelt's proposal to add more justices to the Supreme Court of the United States.
- July 24 – Alabama drops rape charges against the so-called *Scottsboro Boys*.
- July 25–31 – Sino-Japanese War: Battle of Beiping–Tianjin, a series of actions fought around Beiping and Tianjin, resulting in Japanese victory.
- July 28 – The Irish Republican Army attempts the assassination by bomb of George VI in Belfast.
- July 29 – Tungchow Mutiny: units of the East Hopei Army mutiny and kill Japanese troops and civilians in Tōngzhōu.
- July 31 – NKVD operative order 00447 «Об операции по репрессированию бывших кулаков, уголовников и других антисоветских элементов» ("The operation for repression of former kulaks, criminals and other anti-Soviet elements") is approved by the Politburo of the Soviet Union, initially as a 4-month plan for 75,950 people to be executed and an additional 193,000 to be sent to the Gulag.

August

- August 2 – The Marihuana Tax Act Pub. 238, 75th Congress, 50 Stat. 551 (Aug. 2, 1937), is a significant bill on the path that will lead to the criminalization of cannabis. It was introduced to U.S. Congress by Commissioner of the Federal Bureau of Narcotics, Harry Anslinger. (The Act is now commonly referred to using the modern spelling as the 1937 Marijuana Tax Act.)
- August 5 – The Soviet Union commences one of the largest campaigns of the Great Purge, to "eliminate anti-Soviet elements." Within the following year, at least 724,000 people are killed on order of the troikas, directed by Joseph Stalin. This was an offensive that targeted social classes (such as the kulaks), ethnic or racial backgrounds which were seen as non-Russian, and Stalin's

personal opponents from the Communist Party and their sympathizers.
- August 6 – Spanish Civil War: Falangist artillery bombards Madrid.
- August 8 – Japan occupies Beijing.
- August 14 – The Battle of Shanghai.
- August 26 – Second Sino-Japanese War: Japanese aircraft attack the car carrying the ambassador of Great Britain during a raid on Shanghai.

September

- September 2 – The Great Hong Kong Typhoon kills an estimated 11,000 persons.
- September 5 – Spanish Civil War: The city of Llanes falls to the Falangists.
- September 7 – CBS broadcasts a two-and-a-half hour memorial concert nationwide on radio in memory of George Gershwin, live from the Hollywood Bowl. Many celebrities appear, including Oscar Levant, Fred Astaire, Otto Klemperer, Lily Pons and members of the original cast of *Porgy and Bess*. The concert is recorded and released complete years later in what is excellent sound for its time, on CD. The Los Angeles Philharmonic is the featured orchestra.
- September 10 – Nine nations meet in the Nyon Conference, led by the United Kingdom and France, to address international piracy in the Mediterranean.
- September 17 – Abraham Lincoln's head is dedicated at Mount Rushmore.
- September 19 – Swiss professional ice hockey club HC Ambrì-Piotta founded.
- September 21 – George Allen & Unwin, Ltd. of London publishes the first edition of J. R. R. Tolkien's *The Hobbit*.
- September 25 – Second Sino-Japanese War: Battle of Pingxingguan: The Communist Chinese National Revolutionary Army defeats the Japanese.
- September 27 – The last Bali tiger dies.

October

- October 1
  - The Marihuana Tax Act becomes law in the United States.
  - U.S. Supreme Court associate justice Hugo Black, in a nationwide radio broadcast, refutes allegations of past involvement in the Ku Klux Klan.
- October 2–8 – Parley Massacre: Under the orders of President Rafael Trujillo, Dominican troops kill thousands of Haitians living in the Dominican Republic.
- October 3 – Second Sino-Japanese War: Japanese troops advance toward Nanking.
- October 5 – Roosevelt gives his famous *Quarantine Speech* in Chicago.
- October 9 – Jimmie Angel lands his plane on top of Devil's Mountain; however, the plane gets damaged and he has to trek through the rainforest for help.
- October 13 – Germany, in a note to Brussels, guarantees the inviolability and integrity of Belgium so long as the latter abstains from military action against Germany.
- October 15 – Ernest Hemingway's novel *To Have and Have Not* is first published, in the United States.
- October 18–October 21 – Spanish Civil War: The whole Spanish northern seaboard falls into the Falangists' hands; Republican forces in Gijón, Spain, set fire to petrol reserves prior to retreating before the advancing Falangists.
- October 25 – Celâl Bayar forms the new (ninth) government of Turkey.

November

- November 3 – Maurice J. Tobin resoundingly defeats former governor and mayor James Michael Curley in Boston's mayoral election.
- November 5
  - Spanish Civil War – 35,000 Republican supporters are massacred in Piedrafita de Babia, near León.

- o World War II: In the Reich Chancellery, Adolf Hitler holds a secret meeting and states his plans for acquiring "living space" for the German people (recorded in the Hossbach Memorandum).
- November 6 – Italy joins the Anti-Comintern Pact.
- November 9 – Second Sino-Japanese War: Japanese troops take Shanghai.
- November 10 – Brazilian president Getúlio Vargas announces the Estado Novo ("New State"), thence becoming dictator of Brazil until 1945.
- November 11 – The Kogushi sulfur mine collapse, in western Gunma, Japan, kills at least 245 people.

December

December 21: Walt Disney's *Snow White and the Seven Dwarfs* is released, the first full-length traditional-animated feature film, and the first film to feature a Disney Princess. The top image shows the Seven Dwarfs sing "Heigh-Ho" while walking on a log. The second top image shows Walt Disney introducing the Seven Dwarfs in the trailer. The middle image is Snow White, while the bottom images are the trailers.

- December 4 – *The Dandy* comic is first published in Scotland; it will still be running as of 2011.
- December 11 – Italy withdraws from the League of Nations.
- December 12
    - o USS *Panay* incident: Japanese bombers sink the American gunboat USS *Panay*.
    - o Mae West makes a risqué guest appearance on NBC's *Chase and Sanborn Hour*, which eventually results in her being banned from radio.
- December 13 – Second Sino-Japanese War: The Battle of Nanking ends with the Japanese occupying the city. In the Nanking Massacre which follows, Japanese soldiers kill over 300,000 Chinese in 3 months.

- December 16 – The original production of the musical *Me and My Girl* opens at the West End Victoria Palace Theatre in London. A later revival of this musical would win an award.
- December 21 – Walt Disney's *Snow White and the Seven Dwarfs*, the first feature-length traditionally animated film, premieres in selected theaters.
- December 25 – At the age of 70, legendary conductor Arturo Toscanini conducts the NBC Symphony Orchestra on radio for the first time, beginning his successful 17-year tenure with that orchestra. This first concert consists of music by Vivaldi (at a time when he is seldom played), Mozart, and Brahms. Millions tune in to listen, including U.S. President Franklin Delano Roosevelt.
- December 29 – The new Constitution of Ireland (*Bunreacht na hÉireann*) comes into force. The Irish Free State becomes "Ireland", and Éamon de Valera becomes the first Taoiseach (prime minister) of the new state. A Presidential Commission (made up the Chief Justice, the Speaker of Dáil Éireann, and the President of the High Court) assumes the powers of the new presidency, pending the popular election of the first President of Ireland in June 1938. The new constitution prohibits divorce.

Date unknown

- Switzerland begins construction of its Border Line defences.
- The Vibora Luviminda trades union's sugar plantation strike on Maui island, Hawaii.
- Italian psychiatrist Amarro Fiamberti is the first to document a transorbital approach to the brain, which becomes the basis for the controversial medical procedure of transorbital lobotomy.
- John Steinbeck's novella of the Great Depression *Of Mice and Men* is published in the United States.
- Napoleon Hill's self-help book *Think and Grow Rich* is published in the United States.
- Soviet industry produces about four times as much as it had in 1928.

Births

January

Vanessa Redgrave

- January 1 – Anne Aubrey, English actress
- January 4
  - Grace Bumbry, American opera singer
  - Dyan Cannon, American actress
- January 6
  - Paolo Conte, Italian singer, pianist and composer
  - Underwood Dudley, American mathematician
- January 8 – Dame Shirley Bassey, Welsh singer
- January 13
  - George Reisman, American economist
  - Ati George Sokomanu, President of Vanuatu
- January 14
  - Ken Higgs, English cricketer
  - Leo Kadanoff, American physicist (d. 2015)
- January 15 – Margaret O'Brien, American child actress
- January 16 – Francis George, American cardinal (d. 2015)
- January 18
  - Yukio Endo, Japanese gymnast (d. 2009)
  - John Hume, Northern Irish politician; Nobel Peace Prize laureate
- January 19 – Giovanna Marini, Italian singer-songwriter
- January 21 – Prince Max, Duke in Bavaria, heir to the Bavarian Royal House
- January 22 – Joseph Wambaugh, American author

- January 25 – Ange-Félix Patassé, former President of Central African Republic (d. 2011)
- January 27 – John Ogdon, English pianist (d. 1989)
- January 29 – Bobby Scott, American musician, producer and songwriter (d. 1990)
- January 30
    - Vanessa Redgrave, English actress
    - Boris Spassky, Russian chess grandmaster
- January 31
    - Philip Glass, American composer
    - Suzanne Pleshette, American actress (d. 2008)

February

Harald V of Norway

Tom Courtenay

- February 1
    - Don Everly, American rock 'n' roll musician
    - Garrett Morris, American comedian
- February 2

- Remak Ramsay, American actor
- Tom Smothers, American musician and comedian
- Eric Arturo Delvalle, Panamanian lawyer (d. 2015)
- February 3 – Billy Meier, Swiss Prophet
- February 4 – Magnar Solberg, Norwegian biathlete
- February 8
  - Manfred Krug, German actor and singer
  - Harry Wu, Chinese Human Rights activist (d. 2016)
- February 9
  - Francis William Lawvere, American mathematician
  - Robert "Bilbo" Walker Jr., American blues guitarist
- February 10 – Anne Anderson, Scottish physiologist (d. 1983)
- February 11 – Bill Lawry, Australian cricketer
- February 12 – Charles Dumas, American athlete (d. 2004)
- February 13 – Rupiah Banda, President of Zambia
- February 14 – Magic Sam, American musician (d. 1969)
- February 17 – Mary Ann Mobley, American actress; Miss America 1959 (d. 2014)
- February 20
  - Robert Huber, German chemist; Nobel Prize laureate
  - George Leonardos, Greek journalist and author
  - Roger Penske, American race car driver
  - Nancy Wilson, American singer
- February 21
  - Ron Clarke, Australian runner (d. 2015)
  - King Harald V of Norway
- February 25
  - Sir Tom Courtenay, English actor
  - Bob Schieffer, American television journalist

March

Abdelaziz Bouteflika

Warren Beatty

- March 2 – Abdelaziz Bouteflika, President of Algeria
- March 4
  - Graham Dowling, New Zealand cricketer
  - Leslie H. Gelb, American foreign policy expert, President of the Council on Foreign Relations from 1993
  - Yuri Senkevich, Russian cosmonaut (d. 2003)
  - Barney Wilen, French jazz saxophonist (d. 1996)
- March 5 – Olusegun Obasanjo, President of Nigeria
- March 6 – Valentina Tereshkova, Russian cosmonaut, first woman in space
- March 8 – Juvénal Habyarimana, 3rd President of Rwanda (d. 1994)
- March 9 – Harry Neale, Canadian ice hockey coach and broadcaster
- March 14 – Benny Paret, Cuban welterweight boxer (d. 1962)
- March 15 – Valentin Rasputin, Russian writer (d. 2015)

- March 17 – Frank Calabrese, Sr., American gangster in the Chicago Outfit (d. 2012)
- March 20 – Jerry Reed, American country musician (d. 2008)
- March 22 – Armin Hary, German athlete
- March 23
  - Craig Breedlove, American race car driver
  - Tony Burton, American actor and comedian (d. 2016)
- March 27 – Thomas Aquinas Daly, American painter
- March 30 – Warren Beatty, American actor and director

April

Colin Powell

Joseph Estrada

George Takei

Jack Nicholson

Saddam Hussein

- April 5 – Colin Powell, U.S. Secretary of State
- April 6
  - Merle Haggard, American country musician (d. 2016)
  - Billy Dee Williams, American actor
- April 9 – Valerie Singleton, English television presenter
- April 10 – Bella Akhmadulina, Russian poet (d. 2010)

- April 15 – Robert W. Gore, American inventor
- April 16 – George "The Animal" Steele, American professional wrestler
- April 17
  - Don Buchla, American electronic-instrument designer
  - Ferdinand Piëch, Austrian engineer and business magnate
- April 18 – Jan Kaplický, British architect of Czech origin (d. 2009)
- April 19
  - Elinor Donahue, American actress
  - Joseph Estrada, President of the Philippines
- April 20 – George Takei, Japanese American actor, director and author
- April 22 – Jack Nicholson, American film actor
- April 26 – Jean-Pierre Beltoise, French race car driver (d. 2015)
- April 27
  - Sandy Dennis, American actress (d. 1992)
  - Robin Eames, Anglican prelate; Northern Irish clergyman and peace activist
- April 28 – Saddam Hussein, President of Iraq (d. 2006)
- April 29 – Jill Paton Walsh, English novelist

May

George Carlin

Yvonne Craig

- May 1 – Una Stubbs, British actress
- May 2 – Gisela Elsner, German writer (d. 1992)
- May 3 – Hans Cieslarczyk, German football player
- May 4 – Ron Carter, American jazz musician
- May 5 – Trần Đức Lương, President of Vietnam
- May 6 – Rubin "Hurricane" Carter, American boxer (d. 2014)
- May 8
  - Carlos Gaviria Díaz, Colombian justice and politician
  - Thomas Pynchon, American writer
- May 12 – George Carlin, American comedian (d. 2008)
- May 13
  - Trevor Baylis, English inventor
  - Roch Carrier, Canadian writer
  - Roger Zelazny, American writer (d. 1995)
- May 15
  - Madeleine Albright, U.S. Secretary of State
  - Trini Lopez, American musician
- May 16 – Yvonne Craig, American actress (d. 2015)
- May 17 – Hazel O'Leary, U.S. Secretary of Energy
- May 18
  - Brooks Robinson, American baseball player
  - Jacques Santer, Luxembourg politician, President of the European Council
- May 21
  - Sofiko Chiaureli, Georgian actress (d. 2008)
  - John Fairfax, British ocean rower (d. 2012)
  - Mengistu Haile Mariam, former President of Ethiopia
- May 24 – Roger Peterson, pilot who flew the plane on The Day the Music Died (d. 1959)

June

Morgan Freeman

Keizō Obuchi

- June 1
  - Morgan Freeman, American actor
  - Rosaleen Linehan, Irish actress
  - Colleen McCullough, Australian author (d. 2015)
- June 2 – Sally Kellerman, American actress
- June 3
  - Phyllis Baker, American professional baseball player (d. 2006)
  - Crawford Hallock Greenewalt, Jr., American archaeologist (d. 2012)
  - Solomon P. Ortiz, U.S. congressman from Texas
- June 4 – Gorilla Monsoon, American professional wrestler and announcer (d. 1999)
- June 7 –
  - Neeme Järvi, Estonian conductor
  - Roberto Blanco, German singer
- June 8 – Toni Harper, American child singer

- June 9 – Harald Rosenthal, German biologist
- June 10 – Luciana Paluzzi, Italian actress
- June 11 – Robin Warren, Australian pathologist, recipient of the Nobel Prize in Physiology or Medicine
- June 15
    - Herbert Feuerstein, German cabarettist and entertainer
    - Waylon Jennings, American country singer (d. 2002)
    - Alan Thornett, British Trotskyist activist
- June 16
    - Simeon II of Bulgaria, Prime Minister of Bulgaria (2001-2005).
    - Charmian May, British actress (d. 2002)
- June 18
    - Wray Carlton, American football player
    - Vitaly Zholobov, Soviet cosmonaut
- June 19 – André Glucksmann, French philosopher and author (d. 2015)
- June 23 – Martti Ahtisaari, President of Finland
- June 25 – Keizō Obuchi, 54th Prime Minister of Japan (d. 2000)
- June 26 – Robert Coleman Richardson, American physicist, Nobel Prize laureate (d. 2013)
- June 28 – Ron Luciano, American baseball umpire and writer (d. 1995)

July

- July 2 – Richard Petty, seven-time NASCAR Winston Cup champion
- July 4
    - Sonja Haraldsen, Queen of Norway and wife to King Harald V of Norway
    - Wolf von Lojewski, German television journalist
- July 6
    - Vladimir Ashkenazy, Russian pianist
    - Ned Beatty, American actor
    - Michael Sata, Zambian president (d. 2014)

- July 7 – Tung Chee-hwa, Hong Kong administrator
- July 9 – David Hockney, English-born artist
- July 12
  - Bill Cosby, American actor and comedian
  - Lionel Jospin, Prime Minister of France
- July 14 – Yoshirō Mori, 55th Prime Minister of Japan
- July 18
  - Roald Hoffmann, Polish-born chemist, Nobel Prize laureate
  - Hunter S. Thompson, American author and journalist (d. 2005)
- July 20
  - Dick Hafer, American Christian cartoonist (d. 2003)
  - Ken Ogata, Japanese actor (d. 2008)
- July 27
  - Anna Dawson, British actress
  - Don Galloway, American actor (d. 2009)
- July 29
  - Ryutaro Hashimoto, 53rd Prime Minister of Japan (d. 2006)
  - Daniel McFadden, American economist, Nobel Prize laureate

August

Dustin Hoffman

- August 2 – Coenraad Bron, Dutch computer scientist (d. 2006)
- August 4 – David Bedford, American musician (d. 2011)
- August 5 – Herb Brooks, American hockey coach (d. 2003)
- August 6 – Barbara Windsor, English actress
- August 8 – Dustin Hoffman, American actor
- August 14 – Alberta Nelson, American actress (d. 2006)

- August 16
  - David Anderson, Canadian politician
  - Ian Deans, Canadian politician (d. 2016)
- August 18
  - Jean Alingué Bawoyeu, Chadian politician and former Prime Minister
  - Willie Rushton, English comedian and cartoonist (d. 1996)
- August 20
  - Jim Bowen, English stand-up comedian and TV personality
  - Jean-Louis Petit, French composer, conductor and organist
- August 21
  - Donald Dewar, First Minister of Scotland (d. 2000)
  - Robert Stone, American novelist
  - Chuck Traynor, American pornographer (d. 2002)
- August 26
  - Kenji Utsumi, Japanese voice actor and actor (d. 2013)
  - Gennady Yanayev, former Soviet leader (d. 2010)
- August 27 – Alice Coltrane, American jazz harpist, organist, pianist and composer (d. 2007)
- August 29 – James Florio, Governor of New Jersey
- August 30 – Bruce McLaren, Founder of McLaren Racing (d. 1970)
- August 31 – Bobby Parker (guitarist), from USA (d. 2013)

September

- September 4
  - Dawn Fraser, Australian swimmer
  - Mikk Mikiver, Estonian actor and director (d. 2006)
- September 5 – William Devane, American actor
- September 6
  - Kirtanananda Swami Bhaktipada (Keith Gordon Ham), American-born Hare Krishna guru (d. 2011)
  - Jo Anne Worley, American comedian
- September 7 – Cüneyt Arkın, Turkish film actor
- September 10 – Tommy Overstreet, American country singer (d. 2015)

- September 11 – Paola Ruffo di Calabria, Italian-born Queen of the Belgians
- September 13 – Don Bluth, American director, producer
- September 15
  - Jean-Claude Decaux, French advertising executive (d. 2016)
  - King Curtis Iaukea, American professional wrestler (d. 2010)
  - Robert Lucas, Jr., American economist, Nobel Prize laureate
  - Fernando de la Rúa, President of Argentina
- September 16
  - Keith Bosley, British broadcaster, poet and translator
  - David Daker, English actor
- September 17 – Ilarion Ionescu-Galați, Romanian conductor
- September 19 – Abner Haynes, American football player
- September 26 – Jerry Weintraub, American film producer and talent agent (d. 2015)
- September 28 – Rod Roddy, American television announcer (d. 2003)

October

- October 2 – Johnnie Cochran, American attorney (d. 2005)
- October 4
  - Jackie Collins, English author (d. 2015)
  - Franz Vranitzky, former Chancellor of Austria
- October 5 – Barry Switzer, American football coach
- October 11 – Bobby Charlton, English footballer
- October 15 – Linda Lavin, American actress (*Alice*)
- October 17 – Paxton Whitehead, English actor
- October 23 – Carlos Lamarca, Brazilian military turned guerrilla leader (d. 1971)
- October 24
  - John Goetz, American professional baseball player (d. 2008)
  - M. Rosaria Piomelli, born Agrisano, Italian-born American architect
- October 28 – Lenny Wilkens, American basketball player and coach

November

Loretta Swit

Marlo Thomas

Ridley Scott

- November 1
  - "Whisperin" Bill Anderson, American country music singer-songwriter and game show host
  - Witta Pohl, German actress (d. 2011)
- November 2 – Earl Carroll, American lead vocalist for The Cadillacs (d. 2012)
- November 4

- Michael Wilson, Canadian politician and diplomat
- Loretta Swit, American actress
- November 5
  - Chan Sek Keong, third Chief Justice of Singapore
  - Harris Yulin, American actor
- November 6 – Joe Warfield, American actor
- November 8 – Paul Foot, British journalist (d. 2004)
- November 10 – Zdeněk Zikán, Czech football player (d. 2013)
- November 11 – Stephen Lewis, Canadian politician and diplomat
- November 15 – Yaphet Kotto, American actor
- November 17
  - Peter Cook, English comedian and writer (d. 1995)
  - Manuel Félix López, Ecuadorian politician (d. 2004)
- November 20 – Ruth Laredo, American pianist (d. 2005)
- November 21
  - Ingrid Pitt, Polish-born British actress (d. 2010)
  - Marlo Thomas, American actress, producer, and social activist
- November 26 – Boris Yegorov, Russian cosmonaut (d. 1994)
- November 30 – Ridley Scott, British film director

December

Jane Fonda

Sir Anthony Hopkins

- December 1
  - Chuck Low, American actor
  - Vaira Vīķe-Freiberga, former President of Latvia
- December 3 – Bobby Allison, American race car driver
- December 7 – Kenneth Colley, English actor
- December 8
  - Michael Bowen, American artist (d. 2009)
  - James MacArthur, American actor (d. 2010)
  - Arne Næss, Jr., Norwegian mountaineer and businessman (d. 2004)
- December 9 – Darwin Joston, American actor (d. 1998)
- December 11 – Jim Harrison, American writer
- December 12 – Willie Stokes, American mobster (d. 1986)
- December 17 – Kerry Packer, Australian businessman (d. 2005)
- December 21 – Jane Fonda, American actress and social activist
- December 26 – Professor John Horton Conway, mathematician
- December 28 – Ratan Tata, Indian industrialist
- December 29
  - Maumoon Abdul Gayoom, President of the Maldives (1978–2008)
  - Dieter Thomas Heck, German television presenter, singer and actor
  - Barbara Steele, British actress
- December 30
  - Gordon Banks, English footballer
  - John Hartford, American musician and composer (d. 2001)
  - Jim Marshall, American football player
  - Noel Paul Stookey, American singer (Peter, Paul and Mary)

- December 31
  - Avram Hershko, Israeli biologist, recipient of the Nobel Prize in Chemistry
  - Sir Anthony Hopkins, Welsh actor

Date unknown

- Cathie Jung, owner of the smallest waist on a living person (measuring just 15 in.).

Deaths

January

H. P. Lovecraft

- January 1 – Bhaktisiddhanta Sarasvati, Indian spiritual teacher (b. 1874)
- January 2 – Ross Alexander, American actor (b. 1907)
- January 4 – Paul Behncke, German admiral (b. 1869)
- January 6 – André Bessette, Canadian religious leader (b. 1845)
- January 12 – Martin Johnson, American adventurer and documentary filmmaker (plane crash) (b. 1884)
- January 17 – Richard Boleslavsky, Polish film director (b. 1889)
- January 21 – Marie Prevost, Canadian actress (b. 1898)

February

- February 5 – Lou Andreas-Salomé, Russian-born writer (b. 1861)
- February 7 – Elihu Root, American statesman and diplomat, recipient of the Nobel Peace Prize (b. 1845)

- February 11 – Walter Burley Griffin, American architect and town planner (b. 1876)
- February 24 – Guy Standing, British actor (b. 1873)
- February 27 – Charles Donnelly, Irish poet (killed in battle) (b. 1915)

March

- March 8 – Howie Morenz, Canadian ice hockey player (b. 1902)
- March 9 – Paul Elmer More, American critic and essayist (b. 1864)
- March 11 – Joseph S. Cullinan, American oil industrialist, founder of *Texaco* (b. 1860)
- March 12 – Charles-Marie Widor, French organist and composer (b. 1840)
- March 15 – H. P. Lovecraft, American writer (b. 1890)
- March 17 – Austen Chamberlain, English statesman, recipient of the Nobel Peace Prize (b. 1863)
- March 20 – Harry Vardon, English golf professional (b. 1870)
- March 22
    - Alfred Dyke Acland, British military officer (b. 1858)
    - Mary Russell, Duchess of Bedford, English aviatrix and ornithologist (plane crash) (b. 1865)
- March 29 – Karol Szymanowski, Polish composer (b. 1882)

April

Noel Rosa

John Davison Rockefeller

- April 10 – Ralph Ince, American film director (b. 1887)
- April 14 – Ned Hanlon, American baseball manager and MLB Hall of Famer (b. 1857)
- April 16 – Jay Johnson Morrow, American military engineer and politician, 3rd Governor of the Panama Canal Zone (b. 1870)
- April 19 – William Martin Conway, British art critic and mountaineer (b. 1856)
- April 19 – William Morton Wheeler, American entomologist (b. 1865)
- April 21 – Saima Harmaja, Finnish poet (b. 1913)
- April 22 – Arthur Edmund Carewe, Armenian-American actor (b. 1884)
- April 24 – Lucy Beaumont, English actress (b. 1873)
- April 25 – Michał Drzymała, Polish rebel (b. 1857)
- April 27 – Antonio Gramsci, Italian Communist writer and politician (b. 1891)
- April 29
  - William Gillette, American actor (b. 1853)
  - Wallace Carothers, American chemist, inventor of nylon (b. 1896)

May

- May 1 – Snitz Edwards, Hungarian actor (b. 1868)
- May 4 – Noel Rosa, Brazilian songwriter (b. 1910)
- May 6 – 36 victims of the *LZ 129 Hindenburg* disaster.

- May 23 – John D. Rockefeller, American industrialist and philanthropist (b. 1839)
- May 24 – Luis F. Álvarez, Spanish American physician (b. 1853)
- May 25 – Henry Ossawa Tanner, American Artist (b. 1859)
- May 28 – Alfred Adler, Austrian psychologist (b. 1870)

June

J. M. Barrie

- June 2 – Louis Vierne, French composer (b. 1870)
- June 3 – Emilio Mola, Spanish Nationalist commander (plane crash) (b. 1887)
- June 7 – Jean Harlow, American film actress (b. 1911)
- June 10 – Robert Laird Borden, 8th Prime Minister of Canada (b. 1854)
- June 12 – Mikhail Tukhachevsky, Soviet Army officer and Red Army commander-in-chief (executed) (b. 1893)
- June 18 – Gaston Doumergue, 13th President of France (b. 1863)
- June 19 – J. M. Barrie, Scottish novelist and dramatist (b. 1860)
- June 25 – Colin Clive, British actor (b. 1900)

July

Guglielmo Marconi

- July 2 – Amelia Earhart, American aviator (missing on this date) (b. 1897)
- July 9 – Oliver Law, American labor organizer and Army officer (killed in battle) (b. 1899)
- July 11 – George Gershwin, American composer (b. 1898)
- July 13 – Victor Laloux, French architect (b. 1850)
- July 18 – Julian Bell, English poet (killed in battle) (b. 1908)
- July 20 – Guglielmo Marconi, Italian-born inventor (b. 1874)

August

- August 6 – F. C. S. Schiller, German-British philosopher (b. 1864)
- August 11 – Edith Wharton, American writer (b. 1862)
- August 27 – Andrew W. Mellon, American banker and U.S. Secretary of the Treasury (b. 1855)
- August 30 – Tomás António Garcia Rosado, Portuguese general (b. 1854)

September

- September 2 – Pierre de Coubertin, French founder of the modern Olympic Games (b. 1863)
- September 13 – Ellis Parker Butler, American humorist (b. 1869)
- September 14 – Tomáš Garrigue Masaryk, Czechoslovak president (b. 1850)
- September 21 – Osgood Perkins, American actor (b. 1892)
- September 22 – Ruth Roland, American actress (b. 1892)
- September 26 – Bessie Smith, African-American singer (b. 1894)
- September 29 – Ray Ewry, American athlete (b. 1873)

October

Ramsay MacDonald

Ernest Rutherford

Maurice Ravel

- October 16 – Jean de Brunhoff, French writer (b. 1899)
- October 17 – J. Bruce Ismay, English businessman (b. 1862)
- October 19 – Ernest Rutherford, New Zealand physicist, recipient of the Nobel Prize in Chemistry (b. 1871)
- October 26 – Józef Dowbor-Muśnicki, Polish general (b. 1867)

November

- November 6 – Johnston Forbes-Robertson, British stage actor (b. 1853)
- November 9 – Ramsay MacDonald, Prime Minister of the United Kingdom (b. 1866)
- November 11 – Uryū Sotokichi, Japanese admiral (b. 1857)
- November 13 – Caroline Louise Dudley (aka Mrs. Leslie Carter), stage & screen actress (b. 1862)
- November 23 – Miklós Kovács Hungarian Slovene writer (b. 1857)
- November 17 – Jack Worrall, Australian cricketer and coach (b. 1860)
- November 23
  - Jagadish Chandra Bose, Indian physicist (b. 1858)
  - George Albert Boulenger, Belgian naturalist (b. 1858)
- November 25 – Raymond Stanton Patton, American admiral and engineer, second Director of the United States Coast and Geodetic Survey (b. 1882)
- November 27 – Wilhelm Weinberg, German physician (b. 1862)

December

- December 3 – Prosper Poullet, former Prime Minister of Belgium (b. 1868)
- December 8 – Hans Molisch, Czech-Austrian botanist (b. 1856)
- December 9 – Gustaf Dalén, Swedish physicist, Nobel Prize laureate (b. 1869)
- December 12 – Alfred Abel, German actor (b. 1879)
- December 20 – Erich Ludendorff, German general (b. 1865)
- December 21
  - Ted Healy, American actor (b. 1896)
  - Frank B. Kellogg, United States Secretary of State, recipient of the Nobel Peace Prize (b. 1856)
- December 25 – Newton D. Baker, United States Secretary of War (b. 1871)
-

- December 28
  - Herbert Bullmore, Scottish Rugby Union international, grandfather of Kerry Packer (b. 1874)
  - Maurice Ravel, French composer (*Bolero*) (b. 1875)
- December 30 – Hans Niels Andersen, Danish businessman, founder of the East Asiatic Company (b. 1852)

Date unknown

- Paul Behncke, German admiral (b. 1869)
- The 300,000 Chinese in Nanking, the Capital of China.

Nobel Prizes

- Physics – Clinton Joseph Davisson, George Paget Thomson
- Chemistry – Walter Haworth, Paul Karrer
- Physiology or Medicine – Albert von Szent-Györgyi Nagyrapolt
- Literature – Roger Martin du Gard
- Peace – Robert Cecil

In the News

Amelia Mary Earhart mysteriously disappears over the Pacific Ocean during a circumnavigation flight.

Former King OF England King Edward VIII marries Wallis Warfield Simpson on June 3rd.

King George VI becomes the British Monarch when he is crowned on May 12th at Westminster Abbey.

The German airship Hindenburg bursts into flames while attempting to moor at Lakehurst, New Jersey.

Aviator Howard Hughes breaks his own transcontinental flight speed record when he flies from Los Angeles to Newark.

The Emergency 999 Telephone service is started on June 30th in the UK.

Joe Louis nicknamed The Brown Bomber defeats American Jim Braddock on June 22nd.

Japanese forces capture the city of Nanking in China.

Neville Chamberlain becomes the British prime minister.

The Golden Gate Bridge in San Francisco, is opened.

1937 Calendar

January 1937
Sun	Mon	Tue	Wed	Thu	Fri	Sat
					1	2
3	4	5	6	7	8	9
10	11	12	13	14	15	16
17	18	19	20	21	22	23
24	25	26	27	28	29	30
31						

February 1937
Sun	Mon	Tue	Wed	Thu	Fri	Sat
	1	2	3	4	5	6
7	8	9	10	11	12	13
14	15	16	17	18	19	20
21	22	23	24	25	26	27
28						

March 1937
Sun	Mon	Tue	Wed	Thu	Fri	Sat
	1	2	3	4	5	6
7	8	9	10	11	12	13
14	15	16	17	18	19	20
21	22	23	24	25	26	27
28	29	30	31			

April 1937
Sun	Mon	Tue	Wed	Thu	Fri	Sat
				1	2	3
4	5	6	7	8	9	10
11	12	13	14	15	16	17
18	19	20	21	22	23	24
25	26	27	28	29	30	

May 1937
Sun	Mon	Tue	Wed	Thu	Fri	Sat
						1
2	3	4	5	6	7	8
9	10	11	12	13	14	15
16	17	18	19	20	21	22
23	24	25	26	27	28	29
30	31					

June 1937
Sun	Mon	Tue	Wed	Thu	Fri	Sat
		1	2	3	4	5
6	7	8	9	10	11	12
13	14	15	16	17	18	19
20	21	22	23	24	25	26
27	28	29	30			

July 1937
Sun	Mon	Tue	Wed	Thu	Fri	Sat
				1	2	3
4	5	6	7	8	9	10
11	12	13	14	15	16	17
18	19	20	21	22	23	24
25	26	27	28	29	30	31

August 1937
Sun	Mon	Tue	Wed	Thu	Fri	Sat
1	2	3	4	5	6	7
8	9	10	11	12	13	14
15	16	17	18	19	20	21
22	23	24	25	26	27	28
29	30	31				

September 1937
Sun	Mon	Tue	Wed	Thu	Fri	Sat
			1	2	3	4
5	6	7	8	9	10	11
12	13	14	15	16	17	18
19	20	21	22	23	24	25
26	27	28	29	30		

October 1937
Sun	Mon	Tue	Wed	Thu	Fri	Sat
					1	2
3	4	5	6	7	8	9
10	11	12	13	14	15	16
17	18	19	20	21	22	23
24	25	26	27	28	29	30
31						

November 1937
Sun	Mon	Tue	Wed	Thu	Fri	Sat
	1	2	3	4	5	6
7	8	9	10	11	12	13
14	15	16	17	18	19	20
21	22	23	24	25	26	27
28	29	30				

December 1937
Sun	Mon	Tue	Wed	Thu	Fri	Sat
			1	2	3	4
5	6	7	8	9	10	11
12	13	14	15	16	17	18
19	20	21	22	23	24	25
26	27	28	29	30	31	

www.ingramcontent.com/pod-product-compliance
Lightning Source LLC
Chambersburg PA
CBHW061802280526
45787CB00003BA/1444